How to Grow Old Elegantly

Learn the Tricks Your DNA

Has in Store for You

JOSEPH D CAMHI, PhD

CONTENTS

Joseph D. Camhi, PhD

PREFACE ON BIRTH AND AGING

All living systems must carry out their life program going through birth, development, reproduction and aging, and eventually dying.

This e-Book presents in an easy to understand manner some elements of complex science; science that we daily live with and often overlook; the science of growing old in style.

Through a complicated series of events we, humans and all living things, do grow old though the postulate of this book is that growing old does not necessarily means to age.

Aging happens; growing old is more of a mental state mixed with physical conditioning. It's this mental state that we'd like to improve by applying the ideas proposed in this book.

Joseph D. Camhi, PhD

Learning about aging and its relationship with the DNA molecule depicted below has become mandatory to understand our own mysteries.

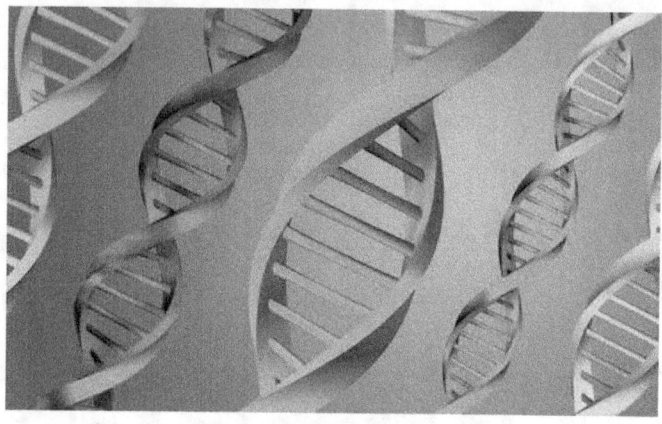

Elegance is a relative term and its meaning in the context of this writing expresses a pleasant and more stylish approach to deal with our body's obligation to age.

Growing old elegantly does not modify our life clock, but can help us deal with aging, a distressing process for most, using a different mental approach.

Joseph D. Camhi, PhD

At the same time, we'll get familiarized with a basic understanding of the human genetic code and its load of information. Information carried from parents to children; data we can read, and many times modify.

The suggestions here offered are not intended to replace formal medical therapy, in instances justified to cause a cure, or minimize an individual's suffering.

Various topics of this e-Book can be studied in more detail using the website addresses suggested in the References page at the end of the book.

Enjoy the reading.

Joseph D. Camhi, PhD

ONE PERSONAL DNA CODE

All the information about who you are and what you are chemically is stored in tiny coiled bits of protein and nucleic acids locked in the nucleus of your cells – all of your cells – except red blood cells that carry the Hem complex of oxygen-hemoglobin-iron, which gives blood its red color.

Hence, all weaknesses and strengths that you may have as an individual are codified in your genes, and that even your behavioral traits, such as aggressiveness and inner peace, are also to a large extent depending on the biochemical configuration of your genes, which you inherited 50% from each of your parents, and they got theirs 50/50 from their parents as well and so forth.

A Gene is the basic unit of heredity and is made of specific segments of a large molecule called deoxyribonucleic acid or DNA, which

Joseph D. Camhi, PhD

carries the genetic information of our body's cells. Genes make up larger structures called chromosomes that will be discussed in another chapter.

Today private laboratories for a fee can establish your personal genetic map and show where the future will take you in terms of risk to develop certain diseases you may develop due to modifications of a particular gene. This is not a desirable exercise as it induces anxiety and fear; "be careful about what you ask for", is true in this case. Certain things you do not need to know.

What you want to know is what you can check on the spot, from what's at hand and can be seen, because reading your inheritance is a different thing. It will help you focus on the good and not be fearful about the surprises that your gene expressions can bring you tomorrow, through lab reports or medical speculation.

Joseph D. Camhi, PhD

Courtesy of photobucket

DNA (deoxyribonucleic acid), this very large and sophisticated molecule, acts as the outline for all the proteins that your body manufactures, thousands of them, all with a particular role and function, and although inheritance is the basic mechanism of

Joseph D. Camhi, PhD

transfer of characteristics of a species, not all inherited traits are irreversible. So when certain types of disease are associated with a specific gene or protein chain in your cells, it does not mean that this disease cannot be reverted under certain conditions and the cells able to be reset to normal functioning, in fact curing the disease.

Observe your parents, your brothers, your family members - young and old - get familiarized with grandparents, cousins, nephews and even your own children, and search like in a genealogical tree traits that are repetitive, typical, which can be anticipated.

This exercise is useful to understand some characteristics that have been transmitted, inherited, because genes repeat themselves as the laws of heredity work their way to improve your chances to survive in a hostile environment. If the environment is too

Joseph D. Camhi, PhD

comfortable, too cozy, giving you a false sense of security, your genes will sense this and won't provide you with the weapons of change for the body or the mind to adapt for the better.

This does not mean that under certain conditions you will not need to resort to complex laboratory testing to evaluate or determine a genetically based disease, but in the simplest of terms, many genetic traits are detectable by just being a keen observer.

Remember, your responsibility is to live as long as you can in a healthy body. Your gene code will help you, but you need to learn to read its meaning. Sometimes the reading can be misleading, often times you won't listen. In the end you can become what you want if you establish who the boss is: Your DNA, your environment, or your brain.

Joseph D. Camhi, PhD

Example: Imagine that your grandmother suffers from back problems and that your mother appears to complain some times of back discomfort, although she is young and fit. Would you not anticipate that your column, your vertebrae, your skeleton, may carry an inbuilt weakness that you need to work on? And although there is a trait of possible weakness, you were alerted by your observation that a life change might be necessary for you to avoid future distress. Implementing a regular exercise program, for instance, to reinforce your back muscles.

In the example above you have just read an important genetic message. You've read your inheritance. Congratulations. Observe, carefully, objectively, any and all the family members you have access to and take note.

Another example: If your grandparents lived to be a hundred, would you expect that of your parents? You think because of this anticipated result, you might become a centenarian as well? Very likely, if you live a similar life to them, in an environment comparable to theirs. Not so, if you practice skydiving, car racing, or are in the Military at war, work in a coal mine, or if your diet is mostly made of hamburgers and ketchup.

In this manner you can learn to read basic traits that could be associated with disease in the future. But mostly you will get a glimpse at what your heredity may bring you: a short or long life; a healthy or sickly existence; a happy mood or a depression; a self-sufficient contentment or a life of dependence.

Remember, when you identify a trait that calls your attention, study it. Read about it; attempt to understand it. You cannot see what is going on at the cellular level, but certain things you can see and evaluate, such as behavior, weight, height, resistance to disease, pain,

Joseph D. Camhi, PhD

allergies, even phobias and talents. Become an observant of traits or the unusual.

To see what others cannot see is called vision. This vision can change the way in which you do things, deal with your life and the way you interact with people, change your mood, your diet and your mental approach to the good and bad that is typical of daily living.

Good. You are now on your way to become the best observant of characteristics that you learned to identify as important.

Complex science with simplicity: In the DNA molecule image below you can see its spatial stringy complexity and the enormous amount of data that it is possible to harness with this configuration. The data is coded within genes and genes code for proteins. It is estimated that there are 10 billion proteins of approximately 10,000 different varieties. Proteins that carry oxygen like hemoglobin;

Joseph D. Camhi, PhD

digest our food like pepsin, make up our hair and nails like keratin, that provide skin elasticity like elastin, that defend us like antibody proteins, that speed chemical reactions like enzymes, and more. The ribonucleic acid or RNA is another complex molecule of that is responsible for translating information, acting as a DNA reader.

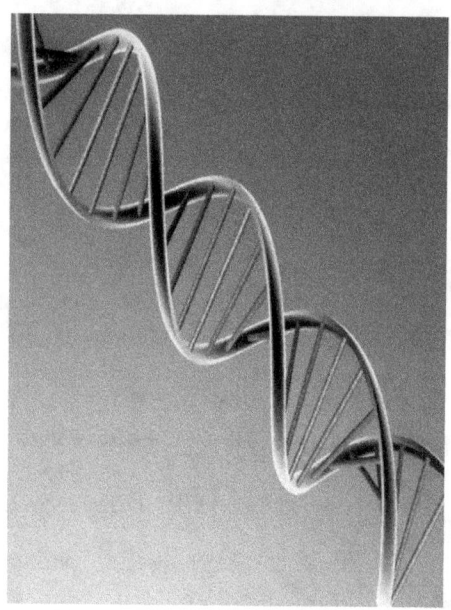

All living organisms contain both DNA and RNA material within their cells. Viruses, which are generally not considered to be living, contain

Joseph D. Camhi, PhD

one or the other. HIV for instance takes over the DNA of the human host and forces it to manufacture more viral particles, thus spreading the viral infection.

Summary: The DNA carries your genetic information and the RNA reads or translates the information inbuilt in the DNA molecule to make specific proteins.

DIFFERENCES IN DNA AND RNA:

In most viruses, RNA is a single chain molecule while DNA is always double-stranded (coiled helix molecule).

The molecules DNA and RNA contain a ribose sugar (a 5-carbon sugar), phosphate groups and FOUR different nitrogen rich smaller molecules, three of which are the same for both RNA and DNA: guanine, adenine and cytosine. Thymine, the fourth molecule which is part of DNA is replaced by the molecule uracil in RNA.

Joseph D. Camhi, PhD

The nitrogen containing molecules: adenine, and guanine are called purine bases, while cytosine, thymine and uracil are called pyrimidine bases. DNA and RNA molecules contain different ribose sugars. DNA has a deoxyribose and RNA a ribose.

The spatial configuration of the DNA helix, shown in this book, is a marvelous piece of molecular architecture that includes an intricate mesh of 5-carbon sugars, and the four (4) nitrogenous bases mentioned above.

It is within this complex structure that our secrets of survival, disease and mechanisms of inheritance are coded.

Again using simple science: In a marvelous and infinitively complicated procedure that defies the imagination, a protein called RNA polymerase splits the DNA molecule into two

Joseph D. Camhi, PhD

strands of RNA, then some of this RNA is used outside the nucleus of the cell to translate the information of the DNA into proteins needed for all biochemical tasks of the body.

In order to unveil the mysteries hidden in the human DNA an international initiative coordinated by the U.S. Department of Energy was implemented in 1990, thus the Human Genome Project (HGP) was born and completed in 1993.

The U.S. Department of Energy and the National Institutes of Health (NIH) coordinated the multidisciplinary effort with the aim to chart all of the DNA contents of the human genome (the sum of all of its DNA and genes).

The Project intended to map all of the approximately three (3) billion nitrogenous bases in the DNA, as well as the about 25,000 genes that make up the genome itself, which we already mentioned codes for about 10 billion proteins of 100,000 varieties.

By the same token, the coordinators also

intended to create a data bank with the information that resulted from the research and to make such database available to the private industry to investigate its commercial potential, as well as to making available its newly developed methods of genome analysis, and finally to consider the legal, ethical and social aspects of the use of this genomic data.

There is no doubt that many of the diseases now haunting humanity will have a solution in the realm of genomic science and in fact today there are a number of biotechnology companies focused in developing new techniques and products that would have an application in resolving common or more uncommon health issues.

The author recommends the References section to learn more about the Human Genome Project and its far-reaching possibilities as well as its life-changing consequences.

19
Joseph D. Camhi, PhD

TWO THE AGING PROCESS

Aging is the process through which our bodies suffer wear and tear by time.

Aging causes a cascade effect of negative events such as dehydration, genetic mutations, immunological incompetence, organ ineffectiveness, reduced intestinal movement, lower protein synthesis, muscular degradation, bone brittleness, thickened heart muscle walls, incompetent bladder, reduced cell division and many more, the end result of which is a disease state that in turn accelerates our biological machinery's failure and deterioration.

HOW AND WHY WE AGE?

Growing old is not merely the passing of time. Aging is a complex event that occurs over a lifetime, making cells to reduce their ability to divide, defend and grow. This complexity may or may not be controlled by us, but surely

Joseph D. Camhi, PhD

learning about its will make us observe it further and perhaps respect it more.

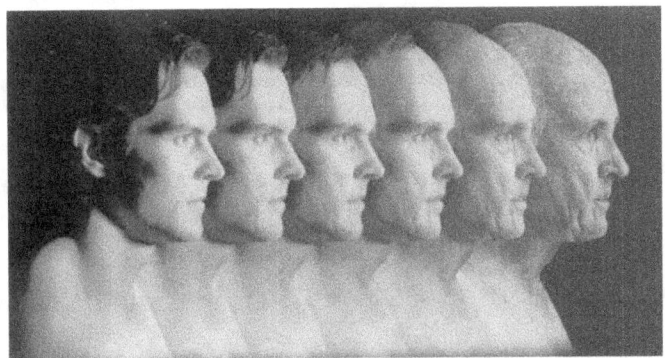

We can see in the example above the effects of time on hair growth, skin elasticity, bone configuration, fat and muscle distribution, eyesight and other, all external manifestations of events happening on the inside of our cells.

ABOUT THE THEORIES OF AGING

The theories of aging revolve around the idea that our genetic material is either pre programmed to die at a certain time or it is changed, mutated over time and that these

Joseph D. Camhi, PhD

abnormal changes eventually trigger or accelerate the process of aging. The chief element involved in these theories in our genetic data bank, the DNA molecule depicted below.

This extraordinary molecule depicted below: the chemical helix shaped structure that holds, among others, the EIGHT SECRETS we are about to uncover in this book.

The DNA molecule stores within its complexity the mysteries of heredity, disease, immunological resistance, intelligence, aptitude, the way we age, the color of our eyes and hair, weaknesses and strengths, physical characteristics, sex, and many more.

We are now opening these secrets to you. Make sure that you follow these simple recommendations about your life's approach,

Joseph D. Camhi, PhD

diet and other various aspects that will be able to change your life for the better.

DNA (deoxy-ribonucleic acid), the double strand helix shaped molecule that contains the code of life and death, present inside the nucleus of all human cells (but red cells) was discovered in 1962 by scientists Watson and Crick, achievement that brought them a Nobel Prize, and represents in this author's concept the most important discovery made by mankind, as it opened the gateway to a fantastic world of possibilities that never ceases to amaze even the most rational or creative of biochemists.

AGING THEORIES ARE OF TWO TYPES

a) Programmed Aging: This theory suggests that aging is a programmed event already preset in our genes; and

b) Gene Error: A theory that proposes environmental damage to our genes

23

through which modifications or mutations of our genetic material accumulate with time inducing the aging process.

There are several variations of the two basic concept theories above, including changes in hormones, immune system decline, rate of oxygen use, free radicals effect, cross-linking of proteins; and wear and tear theory. However, the basic idea remains: Humans age because either genetic mutations cause malfunction at the cellular level or because we are programmed to wear out.

Human cells carry genetic material in their nucleus organized in the form of Chromosomes. There are 46 chromosomes, 23 provided by the female and 23 provided by the male, including the called Y and X sex chromosomes.

Joseph D. Camhi, PhD

So to understand this clearly, the original strands of nucleic acid (DNA) material are organized into genes and the genes themselves are the constituents of chromosomes.

At the end of our chromosomes we have DNA a cap, similar to the ones we see at the end of shoelaces, called Telomeres, which serve a vital function: they protect the endings of the chromosome and repair the damage caused by mutations (radiations, pesticides, and pollutants, UV light and other). The telomeres are long in young (embryonic) stem cells and become shorter in older cells.

When cells divide, the telomeres divide also, getting progressively shorter until cells divide no more and die. This is the basis of one of the Programmed Aging theories: the telomeres divide a fixed number of times and when they cannot continue the process the cells simply

Joseph D. Camhi, PhD

ends its cycle inducing the mechanism of programmed death or apoptosis.

In summary, the number of times our cells divide is dictated by the telomeres, caps of DNA at the tips of human chromosomes, after a defined number of divisions the cell enters into apoptosis (the cell death program is activated) and dies as it cannot replicate anymore.

As stated elsewhere, it's our DNA (in our chromosomes) that holds the secrets of cancer origin and development, and aging; it's DNA that establishes how long we will live or how soon we will die; it's DNA molecule that carries the hereditary traits that will a specific person succeed as a biological system and as an individual, or fail in both endeavors; it's DNA that keeps the secrets of aging well or badly; it is a DNA repair system that eventually can be developed into a true fountain of youth; it's the

Joseph D. Camhi, PhD

DNA that provides us with our inheritance of good or bad genes.

Within the DNA molecules are hidden all of the secrets that we need in order to unveil the cure for cancer and many other diseases, whose origin is genetic. And, of course, how and why we age, as well as how can we interfere with the process.

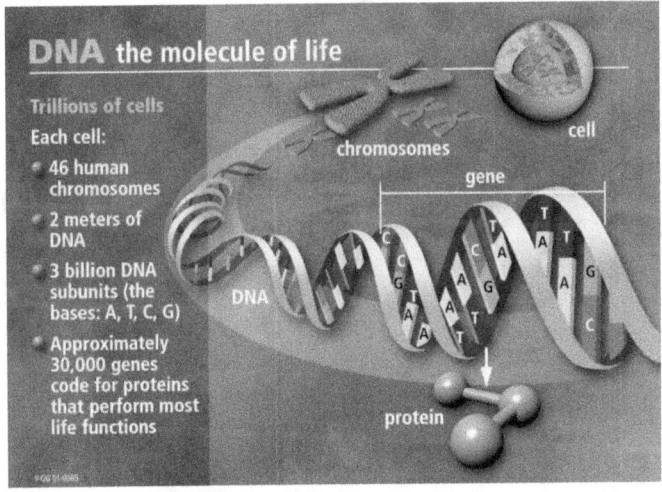

Courtesy of U.S. Department of Energy-Genome Project

In the image above we can see the overall relationship between cell, chromosomes,

Joseph D. Camhi, PhD

genes, the four nitrogen bases, the 5-carbon sugars, RNA and proteins. The command center is in the nucleus of the cell and a type of RNA called messenger or mRNA, now in the cytoplasm translates its code into specific protein chains each one with a biochemical role.

THREE THE ENEMY FROM WITHOUT

The environment to which we are exposed is our first great threat as it continually bombards us with electro magnetic radiation, ultraviolet and infrared waves, industrial chemicals, fumes, carbon monoxide, a multi-variety of pesticides and countless number of solvents, electrical static, as well as other physical and chemical adversaries.

The damage that our environment causes in our almost perfect biological system can vary from unnoticeable skin damage to profound changes in our genetic material, leading to a loss of the equilibrium present in our body's biochemistry, and as a consequence upset the delicate internal balance that challenges our ability to age well.

So what are the causes of these attacks and how do we protect ourselves from enemies from the outside, from our natural world?

HERE ARE A FEW:

Avoid contact with mutagenic chemicals. Sunscreens (PABA, benzophenone), cosmetic creams (parabens, ethylenglycol, and petrolatum) as well as food additives (potassium metabisulphite, potassium sulphate, sodium sulphite, and sodium nitrate) are full of them.

Use Aloe Vera for your skin, as it has multiple benefits as moisturizer and nutrient. For sunscreens use organic natural oil, and avoid the sun between ten in the morning and four in the afternoon. Does this work? Yes, always.

Read the labels of your processed foods or better still avoid their consumption altogether, preferring fresh fruits and vegetables rather than the canned varieties. Avoid cold meat cuts (which contain carcinogenic nitrites) and minimize your consumption of red meat, which takes a long time to transit the digestive

Joseph D. Camhi, PhD

system, develop gases and induce metabolic stress.

Normally the time it takes for food to get processed (from ingestion to passing stools) is 24-72 hours. Natural foods, fruits, raw vegetables, and lean protein will digest faster. Prefer coldwater fish such as wild Alaskan salmon or the less sophisticated canned sardines that contain essential gamma 3 fatty acids (effective anti-inflammatory agents and inducers of HDL - the good cholesterol).

Have sufficient restful sleep – Sleep a minimum of 8 hours. Sleep is our time to recover and in fact the immune system works its best during our slumber hours. Avoid caffeine (coffee, tea or sodas, alcohol or spicy foods) before bedtime, exciting substance that will interfere with profound restful sleep. It's better to go to bed before midnight as it has been proven that melatonin production (a hormone that

Joseph D. Camhi, PhD

facilitates sleep increases before midnight). The ideal time to go to sleep is 10 PM. Lower room temperature to about 65-68 degrees, make the room as dark as possible, use loose cotton clothing, do not eat at least 3 hours before going to bed. Have several small meals during the day in order to stabilize the blood sugar so that you do not crave for food at four in the morning.

Sleep on your back if you can with hands at the side or on your chest. Breathe slowly, eliminate daily problems (sometimes this is an art in itself) from your mind and relax.

Do not eat heavily processed foods Go for fresh organic if you can. Do not put in your mouth anything that is not truly food to generate energy, build muscle, or be a tonic to your internal organs. Go to the website list in References to learn how to select what is best for you, as the foods considered by many to be super-foods.

Reduce levels of stress – Cortisol overproduction by the adrenal glands will cause a mess in your biochemical system. Although the cortisol hormone is produced normally to regulate sugar metabolism, immune function and more, its excess in the blood stream is dangerous.

To relieve stress, anxiety (that on many occasions co-exists with a depressive characteristic) and related conditions, there are easy, available and highly effective ways to control it such as relaxation, imagery exercises, self-hypnosis, physical exercise, or listening to music, strolling by the beach or woods.

Practice meditation – Put aside some quality time for you everyday to just relax and keep your body chemistry in harmony.

Joseph D. Camhi, PhD

Remember that to meditate is not to induce yourself to sleep, in fact it is the art to keep yourself awake and conscious about the relaxation you have induced in your mind, either by just following a specific breathing pattern or concentrating in explicit images that loosen you up.

Take care of your skin - The skin is a reflection of internal health; hence it should be treated with respect. Remember that the skin it's the largest organ of our body. Its functions are many.

1. It protects our internal organs from injury and infection.
2. Detoxifies wastes through perspiration.
3. Provides a barrier to viruses and bacteria.
4. Protects us against extreme changes in temperature.

Joseph D. Camhi, PhD

5. Produces and stores vitamin D, which is vital for cell function.

6. Protects the body from dehydration.

7. Makes us aware of temperature changes around us. And more.

The loss of any of these functions will compromise health and will accelerate the aging process. Besides, the skin also formats our facial expression. Night creams or moisturizers cannot modify an expression of sadness, self-commiseration, ill feeling and defeat. The skin glow must come from within.

Avoid anger. Sometimes this is easier said than done. Anger is like a mist that lingers around us more frequently than it should.

Joseph D. Camhi, PhD

However, anger, prejudice, frustration and self-recrimination will upset your blood pressure and if often practiced, will develop an aura about you that reflects negativity. A constant state of negativity and pessimism reflects an unhappy person. It is better to train yourself to look and act as a happy camper, which is good for you and for those that have to live with you. Nobody stands a sour grape.

Practice laughter. Even when alone, smile; think about a good joke, or a funny episode in your life. Many cultures use group laughter as a therapeutic option, practiced regularly such as martial arts or gymnastics. The best antidote against stress is a good laugh. It relaxes muscles and tension, besides boosting your immune system and inducing the production of the feel-good hormones, endorphins. It is well documented that exercising also increases endorphin production.

Learn Tai Chi Chuan. This ancient Chinese technique - a martial art - is excellent for

Joseph D. Camhi, PhD

relaxing body and mind by using slow, circular movements while focusing on your breathing. Good for the bones, for inner peace, for strengthening and stretching of the muscles and to enhance equilibrium. However, to begin practicing Tai Chi when your spirit is in turmoil is not an easy task, but after a few sessions it becomes easier and the results noticeable.

Protect yourself from the constant threats of the environment by screening what you eat, what do you expose yourself to; what you do with your spare time, how you deal with other people and how integrated is your body with your mind.

Great solutions exist today in the form of tapes, videos and books to teach you how to better interact with your inner self: imagery, meditation, self-hypnosis, yoga, subliminal music and more. But remember: You must want to change; if there is no will to modify your behavior all shall remain the same. To

Joseph D. Camhi, PhD

expect that change will come by repeating the same mistakes every day is foolish.

Remember the basics: everything out there is dangerous and can threaten our lives, from a stupid accident to a viral infection. Millions of bacteria populate the air, our skin and our body; all kept at bay because our sentinel immunological army is always on the prowl for enemies, swiftly attacking, engulfing, neutralizing and destroying any antigen that threatens us. All of this, of course, occurs provided our immune defense system is competent and working to expectation.

If poor sleep, stress, bad nutrition and lack of exercise make part of your life, you can surely expect less than stellar performance from your immune army to defend and protect you effectively.

In conditions of neglect like those described above, our body quickly falls prey to disease

Joseph D. Camhi, PhD

and once sickness sets in a reversal to health can be costly, in both time and money. If the body is weakened it will fight a losing battle to defend itself.

FOUR THE ENEMY FROM WITHIN

Our body, a fantastic universe of more than 100 trillion cells, 22 internal organs, 11 different systems, 600 muscles and 206 bones, is marvelously well organized to perform thousand of simultaneous biochemical reactions to support its role of survival and adaptation; keeping us in this manner in a healthy state, until we deteriorate with age, and die to begin another cycle. Deterioration commences from the inside out and this is where we will have a peek.

Our aim, in fact the aim of our bio-system, should be to age slowly and deteriorate (grow old) unnoticeably. Our behavior though, challenges this order, and often with our actions we precipitate the aging process and its subsequent decay.

Although our body is a perfectly integrated system of cells and organs working together

Joseph D. Camhi, PhD

for our health, there are adversaries we need to constantly fight. These enemies which originate from within ourselves - from inside our own cells are capable of upsetting the chain of command in the instructions given by our genetic code to produce proteins, degrade chemicals, or modify the behavior of specific cells.

WHO ARE THESE ENEMIES?

Cancer is our greatest enemy from within. When certain cells begin to grow unchecked, without control, eventually creating chaos in our body, destroying organs, overwhelming healthy cells and finally taking over to destroy their host, we are in the presence of our most terrible foe.

In the current medical arsenal to deal with this cellular chaos only exists surgery, chemo and radiation – the trio from Hell - which in most cases makes cancer treatment worse than the

Joseph D. Camhi, PhD

cure, as remission of the disease is common, or the treatment leaves sequels and side effects that prove fatal, or induce other types of malignancy.

The word cancer has been associated for a long time with suffering and death. Its name originates from the Greek word for crab, as the ancients thought that some lesions they observed looked much like a crab shape. Today, however, the tendency is to use the word oncology to describe the origin, diagnosis and treatment of a wide range of diseases identified as cancer.

The word oncology is much less intimidating and can even sound hopeful. But do not get deceived; once DNA (genetic) mutations begin in your body, and induce malignance, you must deal with the problem. The ideal case is to never have to face a mutation in our genetic code and this book will help you exactly how to do that. Avoid cancer by using your own DNA strengths.

The lymphatic system is the main component of our biological defense structure. Lymph nodes are small lumps that carry lymph fluid throughout the body. These nodes are located most prominently in the throat, groin and armpit. Lymph fluid contains lymphocytes and other white blood cells and circulates through all the body.

The lymphatic system bathes the cells and acts as a collecting system for waste filtering including viruses, bacteria, cell metabolites, toxins, and eliminates them through the urine, sweat and other excretory mechanisms. When a lymph node is swollen it means it is filtering toxic material or an infective microorganism to attempt to wash it out of the body.

The TWO methods the body uses to impulse the lymphatic fluid to move and reach the points of discharge to get rid of the waste material it carries, is by muscular activity, either walking or breathing.

The lymphatic fluid represents almost 4 times the volume of blood we have circulating, and blood has the benefit of having the heart as a pump to force it to circulate. There is no pump for the lymphatic fluid, so the only way to move it and keep the lymph circulating, eliminating toxins, cellular debris and broken proteins is by moving and breathing.

Purposeful Walk-Breathing: Doing 10 minutes or so of walking briskly and at the same time breathing in and out using an equal count, for example six seconds to inhale and six seconds to exhale will help moving the lymph, and therefore move out the waste your body produces. Experiment six short air intakes through the nose and exhale six short times through the mouth. Try to pace the breathing with your walking. You will feel the difference in your energy level and well being after a few days of practicing.

Deep Energy Breathing: This breathing, which has a marked effect on well being and energy levels as well, is a different technique to force lymph fluid to move around and dispose of its toxic load. It is an inhale-hold-exhale type exercise done in the sequence 1:4:2, ratio found to be effective to maximize results.

Only the ratio is important not the actual numbers, therefore you can inhale for a count of 5, hold for a count of 20, and exhale for a count of 10. This action of inter-coastal muscles, abdominal muscles and the lungs, force the lymph to move.

Normally our lungs exhale air very quickly and the aim should be to at least to double the time of exhaling compared to the inhaling of air. This forces the inter-coastal muscles to work more effectively as the lungs take more time and effort to eliminate the air put on hold.

Joseph D. Camhi, PhD

Do this 3 times a day (morning, midday and evening) ten times on each occasion. You will note a difference in your energy level; you will relax mind and soul, and also protect yourself against aging prematurely.

An advice: Breathe using the Yogic Tongue Position to maximize energy flow, that is: place the tip of the tongue of the hard ridge tissue behind your teeth palate and keep it there until your breath-work is done.

Remember, breath-work is the single most important activity you can do on behalf of your health. It is simple, easy, free and effective; and has been practiced for thousand of years by ancient civilizations.

All cancer is a genetic disease. As stated above, cancer has to do with mutation, change of our DNA, our genetic design, which acts as the commander-in-chief of our biochemical expression. Therefore, be always aware of the

Joseph D. Camhi, PhD

external or internal conditions that may eventually make your DNA mutate. Smoking, alcohol, drugs, radiation, chemicals, pollution, diet, stress, anxiety, and exposure to industrial chemicals are all on the prowl to detect a weak spot.

Autoimmune disease. In some instances there are conditions where our sentinel immune system, (which is in charge to defend us from external invaders), suddenly goes haywire and begins producing antibodies against its own host, ourselves, assailing its own house, such as in the case of Arthritis and Lupus Erythematosus two well-known autoimmune diseases that attack the joints, skin and other organs.

The characteristic of an autoimmune condition is that the immune system malfunctions, so it cannot distinguish between its own body cells and tissues and those foreign particles represented by viruses, bacteria, chemicals, or other invaders. Thus the immune system, developed to protect us, becomes in fact an inner enemy creating antibodies that attack our own organs and tissues and eventually we may end up defeated by our defenses.

Free radicals. As a consequence of energy production inside of our cells (in a process called cellular respiration within intracellular structures known as mitochondria) and the multiple biochemical reactions our body generates free radicals, which are unstable molecules within our bodies that attack (oxidize) and destroy healthy cells making them vulnerable to disease and death. The lethal effects of oxygenation brought about by these free radicals can be countered by the use of antioxidant compounds.

Antioxidants can be water or fat soluble, and it is convenient to include in our diet a mixture of the two types. The free radical scavengers that we need to include in our diet are:

Joseph D. Camhi, PhD

Vitamin E has a protective effect on the heart, reduces oxidation of fats decreasing the amount of LDL (low density lipoprotein, the bad component of cholesterol in the blood, which is responsible for hardening of the arteries.

Vitamin A, the precursor of beta carotene is a powerful remover of free radicals as well;
Vitamin C is widely accepted as an effective antioxidant and an immune system supporter.
Vitamin D has been recently described as an excellent immune system modulator and anti cancer, and protector against diabetes, as every organ in the body has receptors for Vitamin D. Sunrays (UV light) help the formation of Vitamin D in our body.

The minerals Selenium and Zinc that act as enzyme co-factors and facilitate the uptake and maintenance of Vitamin E in the blood; the well known CoQ10 (co-enzyme Q), which is vital in generating intracellular energy;

Joseph D. Camhi, PhD

SOD (super oxide dismutase) and glutathione both powerful removers of oxygen molecules, and other compounds such as Melatonin that facilitates sleep, protects nuclear DNA and activates glutathione peroxidase (an important oxygen-breaker enzyme) as well as DHEA, involved in the origin of all steroid hormones in the body, and an excellent hormonal support.

Alfa lipoic acid, which enhances the effects of glutathione, vitamin E and Vitamin C. So the corollary is: Always consume water and fat & water soluble antioxidants for maximum protection.

Parasites can infest our bodies and station themselves in the intestinal tract feeding themselves of our food and even from our tissues. Eventually these worms will overwhelm our bodies inducing serious disease, weight loss, abdominal pain, fever, bleeding and other. Make a habit of always washing your foods with plenty of clean water, or with a weak solution of bleach to remove contaminants. Lemmon juice and diluted vinegar are also good options.

Bacteria can be bad and good to have living with us. Those nasty bacteria that invade our bodies and proliferate within us as consequence of an infection are normally dealt with by our immune system, sometimes aided by antibiotics if reinforcement is needed.

The good bacteria, of which we have a large population in our intestinal tract are, nevertheless, essential to our existence because they manufacture vitamins – which normally humans cannot make – among which the B complex and in particular vitamin B12, vital for food absorption. These vitamins, also called co-enzymes, are vital for the activity of enzymes (enzymes are proteins with the ability to accelerate a chemical reaction) all of which are very specific in their action. A catalyzer is an element or molecule (metal, vitamin or cofactor) that accelerates the course of a biochemical reaction by helping the protein-enzyme to perform more effectively.

For example the enzyme steroid 5-alfa reductase is responsible for the reaction that transforms Testosterone into DHT (dehydrotestosterone).

DHT is the main factor in the enlargement of men's prostate gland, a condition known as BPH (benign prostate hyperplasia), a medical condition associated with symptoms such as urgency to urinate, incontinence, poor urine flow, difficulty in passing urine, and other nuisances.

The cofactor that drives the enzyme to transform testosterone into DHT is called NADPH (hydrogenated nicotinamide di-phosphate); and the traditional inhibiting factors used to block the enzyme activity (and reduce prostate enlargement or BPH) are chemicals such as Vitamin D3, the metal Zinc,

Joseph D. Camhi, PhD

the herb Saw Palmetto (Serenoa repens) and synthetic drugs such as Finesteride (Proscar) or Dutasteride (two drugs that carry a wide spectrum of dangerous side effects).

FIVE YOU ARE WHAT YOU EAT

You are what you eat, indeed, or better still: you become what you eat, as what you ingest can be vital or deadly. The single most dramatic effect on our health is achieved by what we eat, be it conventional foods grown under a pesticide containing environment, or an intake of organically grown food that spares your body from the toxic effects of agro-chemicals, freeing your DNA from the impact of mutation, cancer development or accelerated aging.

Follow these simple rules to maximize your energy production, to slow aging to a pace that you can handle and minimize damage to your precious genes.

Your parents and grandparents may have left you a fortune in survival genes, 'good genes', which will help you, but if they didn't, you have

Joseph D. Camhi, PhD

to do your own effort to make the best out of you've got.

SO, DO NOT FORGET TO:

Drink water regularly – up to 2 liters a day. Use clean spring water, not tap water (which is full of impurities and chemical contaminants). This will keep your biochemical reactions working in the right environment; your body will be properly hydrated, (this is important because only mild dehydration will be noticeable reducing your energy and disposition).

Water will also control your body temperature, which varies very little around 37 degrees Celsius (98 degrees Fahrenheit).

Properly hydrated your skin will be supple, joints will be lubricated and the body will flush toxins that need to be removed; water also carries nutrients to the cells and provides a moist environment for your throat and nose.

Remember that about sixty percent of the human body is composed by water, which represents the largest chemical component in our biological system, so make a habit of drinking water regularly.

As we lose water daily through breathing, perspiration, urination, bowel movements and other means, which can amount up to 2 liters (urine alone is about 1.5 liters/day), this amount of about 2 liters or 8-9 cups consumption per day will replenish our fluid loss effectively.

Eat Good Foods: Do not gorge yourself with food for the sake of eating, do not use excess salt, condiments or sauces, but rationalize your feeding for better health. Forget about big portions and surplus fat in quickie restaurants on your way home or at the lunchtime break. It's well known that a lean body has more

Joseph D. Camhi, PhD

years to live. And is significantly less stressful to your genes.

Several small portions a day is better than two large meals spaced during 8-10 hours. Do not have iced beer or cold water with your food, as it dilutes the gastric juices. Have warm tea instead, green or oolong teas, which facilitate digestion. The Chinese have been doing this for thousands of years and they do not suffer the maladies we daily live with in our Western civilization.

Green tea was proven to enhance apoptosis, the mechanism by which a cell is programmed to die. Cancer cells have defective apoptosis and live forever; therefore to boost apoptosis is to increase cancer cell death, a therapy currently under trial at a major research institution.

Include fruits and vegetables in your daily formula. Always? Yes, always. Why? Because

Joseph D. Camhi, PhD

this type of foods is rich in vitamins, antioxidants and soluble fiber that will help your metabolism to achieve peak performance, as well as maintaining stools soft and regular without feeling bloated. Keep an organic apple always at hand.

It is well known that broccoli; Brussel sprouts and cauliflower contain powerful antioxidants (of the sulphorane type). Other greens (the greener the better) provide us with additional weapons to defend ourselves from damaging free radicals and oxidative molecules. Do not mix greens with pasta, but preferably eat them with lean meats (poultry, veal or other) to improve protein digestion and maintain proper blood pH balance.

Remember to consider the Glycemic Index of the foods you eat. This index reflects how quickly a sugar is degraded and reaches the blood risking dangerous variations in our blood sugar levels.

Complex carbohydrates (starches) digest more slowly, such as beans, oats, brown rice and integral pasta; others yield glucose in the blood rapidly, which make them undesirable (cakes, muffins, pancakes and the like) and dangerous.

Free sugar (sucrose, fructose syrup, or the like) is detrimental as it metabolizes at high speed in the gut generating not only energy but also a lot of gas, forcing the pancreas to produce extra insulin, and also it's the food by excellence of cancer cells.

Cancerous tissue loves sugar and takes up glucose rapidly to divide and grow not using oxygen, using an anaerobic pathway. The aerobic route to oxidation is the pathway a healthy cell will choose to yield energy. Hence, to maintain the body cells oxygenated (by exercising, deep breathing and other) will keep the body at its best.

Fish, especially cold water fish, is in a different league because its protein has a more easy to metabolize amino acid composition and besides are rich in highly beneficial essential gamma fatty acids (which the human body cannot synthesize), that will protect the heart, cell membranes and internal tissues, including the increase of the good HDL cholesterol.

Eggs, white cheeses, milk, all organically produced if possible, and integral breads are also a necessary part of our diets because they are rich in essential fatty acids, protein, calcium and magnesium minerals as well as insoluble fiber, the latter one specifically used as roughage to enhance intestinal movement (peristalsis).

Joseph D. Camhi, PhD

Therefore as a summary: every age related issue from slower brain activity, through memory loss, wrinkling of the skin, to age spots, can be traced to two basic biochemical activities: oxidation and inflammation.

Hence, eating foods with both antioxidant content and those that also present anti-inflammatory properties will protect you against these two culprits.

For antioxidant chemicals always choose fruit and vegetables that present intense colors such as red, green, orange and yellow.

For foods containing anti-inflammatory properties choose oily fish such as salmon, sardines, and mackerel (tuna is also a good choice), which are rich in omega-3 fatty acids. Oily fish regular consumption also protects against prostate cancer.

Joseph D. Camhi, PhD

Omega 3s is also present in olive oil, flaxseed, avocados, and walnuts. These anti-inflammatory fats protect the heart and enhance brain function, as well as increase the levels of HDL, the good cholesterol.

SIX OUR DEFENSE MECHANISM

Your main mechanism of defense is the immune system, complex, effective and deadly to foreign invaders. Its logistic is so perfect that it is a wonder that this faultless mechanism is not otherwise impaired by the many challenges we face every second we breathe; and unfortunately when it does become inefficient, we turn vulnerable and extremely fragile as the attackers take over the fortress from which our defenses manage to keep them at bay.

Check your lifestyle, which eventually will reinforce or defeat the immune response to protect us. A life style that helps support the immune system is one that overall will make us live longer and better. Your style will include exercise for proper muscle tone and oxygenation, adequate food intake, an equilibrated mind, a body free from stress and

Joseph D. Camhi, PhD

the lack of selfishness to treat you and others with care, consideration and respect.

Have a higher expectation of life, and to be able to communicate with a higher entity, even if invented, for the sake of a communion with your inner self and the creator, if you need to believe, or seeking a master order if you are a non believer. Whatever your religion, whatever you believe in, or a personal philosophical endeavor, it will help to guard you from the negative influences of the environment.

In our human society evil coexists with the good and we shouldn't forget that what a human brain is capable of thinking; it is also capable of achieving, ideally for the better.

Therefore, try every day to develop in your personality, your mind, positive characteristics that will get you nearer to what you think you should be, and that you can be if you want.

Joseph D. Camhi, PhD

This is an obvious advice, but how difficult to implement and fulfill. Lonely and hard work indeed, but if you succeed you'll be self-sufficient.

Avoid Negative People. Other people can be as toxic as any chemical or poison. They are sour, despondent, bitter, aggressive, and sad; and blame the rest of the world for their unhappiness. Although they may have good reasons for their anger they chose not to change and walk through life distilling their frustration. These individuals are easily recognizable. Avoid them.

Learn something new for your self-satisfaction only; from learning to play an instrument to writing a diary. This will force you to detach from the environment, from problems, anxieties and uncertainties that may haunt you. Try it and you'll develop a new private world.

Be distrustful of the human nature, but do not be critical. A dose of cynicism is good. The least you expect from others in terms of kindness or understanding the better. This doesn't mean acting negative or pessimistic, but simply to take things at face value without being too generous. Some people can easily forgive or condemn. It's better to do neither. If you become judgmental about anything it will take time of your precious life. Avoid it.

Have you noted how psychotherapy works? You talk and the therapist listens. He doesn't get involved. As soon as you're out of his office he'll forget about you, without an impact on his life. You are just a profit center and he forgot you until the next session.

Put Money in the right context. Disregard those that preach that money doesn't bring you happiness or is the root of evil. These guys probably already have plenty or none of it. The fact is that wealth is good and the truth is that we live in a society where money brings you privilege and the lack of it humbles you to insignificance.

Worrying about debt that can't be repaid will only accelerate your aging process. The stress hormone Cortisol will flare up distressing you, increasing blood pressure, making you irritable and anxious; and finally bringing disease to knock at your door.

There is no point in implementing a plan for longevity if you must deal daily with a demon as destructive as this.

Have a Pet. It's well known that furry friends are exceptional at providing companionship, regulating your mood better than drugs and being great at social support and also excellent listeners (better than humans). It's said that the dog is man's best friend because it wags its tail more than its tongue, a true statement.

Joseph D. Camhi, PhD

Pets, like dogs especially, give you unconditional love and affection. Get one.

Have meaningful dialogue with others. When talking to other people pay attention to what they say. Most people use sentences that mean nothing, their dialogue full of echoes and empty sentences. Make the exchange meaningful, be sincere in your appreciation, and don't make dialogue for the sake of chitchat. If it becomes pointless cut it short. It's a waste of life.

Daily life dialogue is boring, try to make it interesting. Sometimes silence is truly made of gold.

Protect your DNA.

Avoid interaction with nasty people

Stroll in the sunlight

Watch a good movie

Read an entertaining book

Listen to relaxing music

Go out shopping

Joseph D. Camhi, PhD

Treat yourself to red wine

Drive a convertible

Do not eat junk food

Include antioxidants in your diet

Play chess with your computer

Wear cotton clothes

Sleep in a dark room

Do breath-work every day

Keep your skin moist

Get near people that are in love

Walk by the sea

Thank God everyday

Learn something often

Give anonymously

Talk to children

Say thank you often

Learn a good joke

Joseph D. Camhi, PhD

SEVEN HOW TO PREVENT CANCER

The most important fight of our lives is to keep our bodies free of malignant cells. When a normal cell multiplies abnormally due to mutation, damaged cells build up to form a tumor; if not treated this tumor can break out to other parts of the body originating more tumors and disrupting the functioning of organs. When malignant tumor cells spread in the body, through the blood or the lymphatic fluid, it's said that cancer has metastasis.

Malignancy is the number one killer in the civilized world and attacks young and old, irrespective of sex or ethnicity, bringing disaster to individual lives and families.

Few realize that malignancies are preventable and have much to do with the manner in which we live as well as our genetic weaknesses and strengths.

Joseph D. Camhi, PhD

HOW DO WE PROTECT OURSELVES FROM ACQURING CANCER?

Include cancer fighters in your diet.

An antioxidant is a type of chemical entity that neutralizes free radicals in our body. Free radicals – also called oxygen scavengers - are unstable molecules that cause damage to normal tissue, which can give origin to cancer. Antioxidants are present in blueberries and other similar, such as strawberries and raspberries.

Raspberries in particular are high in **Elagic Acid**, a well-known cell protector. Antioxidants are present in the entire spectrum of fruits, vegetable, nuts, grains and other foods, thus the need to a mixed diet.

Antioxidants are also present in dark chocolate (rich in antioxidant flavonoids), red wine (containing the potent oxygen scavenger

Joseph D. Camhi, PhD

resveratrol), black grapes, navy and red beans; pecan nuts (rich in gamma-tocopherol; a strong Vitamin E form), tomatoes (rich in lycopene); and Brazil nuts (abundant in selenium a metal with strong antioxidant activity). Pecans, for example, contain as much antioxidant activity as two glasses of red wine. Keep some of these nuts handy.

Consume Fiber Every Day

As mentioned elsewhere fiber can be soluble or insoluble. Regardless of its type the best manner to protect your gut against Colon Cancer is regular consumption of fiber, which will enhance intestinal movement and diminish transit time of food, providing regularity in the passing of feces. Raw fruits and vegetables are fiber rich and should make part of your daily diet.

When eating fruits like pears, apples or grapes always choose organic products.

As damage to the colon, the top part of the intestine, can start early in life, it's advised to

Joseph D. Camhi, PhD

begin consumption of at least 30 grams of fiber per day when you are younger in order to promote digestive health in later life. You can use over the counter products such as Psyllium husk, a bulk forming natural fiber, if your dietary consumption is fiber deficient. Psyllium as a natural water absorber needs plenty of fluid to achieve maximum result. Make sure to drink sufficient water when ingesting it.

Always eat apples, pears, plums, plums, nectarines, and other fruits (preferably organic) without peeling to increase your natural fiber intake. Remember the recommended intake of five (5) servings of fruits per day to satisfy your antioxidant requirements.

Men Should Consume Lycopene

As prostate cancer is the most common malignancy in men, it is advisable that the consumption of this important cancer-fighting agent be made regular. Lycopene has been proven to be an effective protector of the incidence of prostate cancer as well as reduce tumor size. Its effect is mostly due to its antioxidant nature. Lycopene is a carotenoid compound, which provides red, yellow and orange color to fruit and vegetables. The highest concentration of lycopene antioxidant is found in tomatoes, watermelon, apricots, grapefruit and other similar sources.

Lycopene is a fat-soluble compound and therefore it is better to cook tomatoes in olive oil, for instance, to maximize its absorption by the intestine. Tomato ketchup is also a good source of this extraordinary product and research on it continues in order to verify its protective effect in other types of malignant conditions.

Quit Smoking Now

The single most valuable decision to affect your health is to never smoke cigarettes and if you do abandon the habit immediately.

Joseph D. Camhi, PhD

Cigarette smoking is the cause of the most common cancer of all: Lung Cancer which touches and destroys the lives of thousands of people every year around the world.

Beware of the Sun.

The sunlight or exposure to it can be your friend or the deadliest foe, as direct sun irradiation over an unprotected skin will not only burn the surface epithelial cells, but UV light will penetrate deeper below the surface reaching into the cells genetic material causing mutations and malignancies, such as deadly melanoma (skin cancer).

A dose of sunlight is beneficial (before 10 am and after 4 pm, when the sun rays are not perpendicular and the UV radiation is less). It's needed to activate the production of Vitamin D, a vital product for our bones resistance and support of the immune system.

Joseph D. Camhi, PhD

Even at the times suggested above it is always recommended to use some type of UV radiation filter in the form of lotion or sunscreen cream.

Sleep in the Dark

Melatonin, a hormone produced in our brain while we sleep, is an important biochemical modulator and also a strong anti-cancer agent.

It has been demonstrated that the incidence of cancer in individuals that do not follow a normal sleep pattern in a dark environment, produce less melatonin and may have a higher incidence of malignancies versus those that sleep at least an 8 hour cycle in full darkness.

Also, melatonin supports the immune system, which mostly works and recovers while we sleep. So the better we sleep the better our immune system will function.

So if you cannot make your room completely dark, be sure to use a sleep mask to darken your perceived space. Sleep deprivation is the source of many health problems.

Give up Alcohol

Today the medical establishment recommends 1 or 2 glasses of red wine per day to their cardiovascular patients. The fact is that alcohol, even in tiny quantities, is extremely toxic to the liver and other organs, such as pancreas and throat.

Distilled spirits such as whiskey and vodka have a high alcohol concentration of about 70%, with wines being in the range of 12 % and beer at an average of 4%. This means that drinking similar amounts of either of these beverages will provide a very different amount of ethanol into the bloodstream of the drinker.

Regardless of the justification to drink alcohol, beyond one glass of wine with a meal because of its antioxidant content, it is a toxic drug, especially to liver and pancreas. As a recreational beverage, ethanol, in any of its

Joseph D. Camhi, PhD

forms is the cause of countless medical conditions varying from hepatitis through cirrhosis to cancer.

Avoid Processed Foods

Processed foods carry synthetic colors, flavoring agents and preserving agents, as well as compounds such MSG, trans-fatty acids, and rancid (oxidized) fats. Also they may contain hormones, either animal or synthetic, sugars like glucose (the main food of cancer cells) or high fructose syrup and more. Pesticides are commonly present in fruits like fruit juices and several fruits, and have been recognized as the causative agents of lymphoma and other types of cancer.

EIGHT GOD AND LONGEVITY

We begin our journey towards aging the moment we are born. Indeed, as the characteristics inherited from our parents show up to facilitate or hinder our personal progress, little importance is given to the fact that we started growing old from the moment of our birth and that it is now our personal responsibility to make the most of what lies ahead.

As a summary, we mentioned throughout this e-book the many aspects that help us to protect ourselves from the environment and the laws that force us through the path of aging, among them our diet, our mental attitude and expectations, the reinforcement of our natural defenses, the development of new weapons to fight the common foes inside and outside of us, the use of antioxidants to fight free radicals that cause damage to our cells, and several other.

Joseph D. Camhi, PhD

However, one important resource that can be used to ensure success in the effort of growing old elegantly is the practice of a belief.

Whether you have a religious belief or are an atheist the reality of life is that aging is a trip traveled alone; therefore the role of family friends and acquaintances and play a vital role in providing the necessary social support needed to accept the process of aging as part of living and not necessary a condition that should be treated as a disease.

However, in many instances this nearby social support does not exist and growing old can become a lonely experience, a stage of life that we fear and that we do not look forward to.

Consequently depression and anxiety can set in, in turn opening the door to disease. In fact the norm for women and men of old age is a depressive condition.

Although we do have only one life to live, growing old should at least give us the wisdom from considerable past experience. Unfortunately this not the rule and only we when we study centenarians we discover some of the personality traits that are necessary to live longer and better.

Optimism:

Those that reach a ripe age in good health share a positive state of mind and have an enthusiastic attitude towards life.

Optimistic people in general live longer than the pessimistic.

Belief and Spirituality:

Spirituality can include meditation and prayer; however it's the belief in God which is the most beneficial. Studies have shown that individuals that attend a house of worship once a week can add years to their lives, and that the idea of God provides hope to continue an active, healthy existence. It is less stressful to believe

Joseph D. Camhi, PhD

in a superior being and trust in a God that cares and controls the events of our lives for the good of us.

Mental Activity:

As we age our mental faculties are challenged, however the long lived keep themselves busy with games, chess, writing poetry, reading, instrument playing or engaging in conversation. The brain requires use. Remember that the mind is a question of either using it or losing it. A mind at rest is a prescription for dementia. Hence, keep your mind busy.

Sense of Humor:

A fundamental characteristic of older people that age successfully is a sense of humor, as humor requires mental and verbal sharpness. Humor also carries laughter with it, which in itself is an excellent exercise and is an excellent tonic for the immune system.

In summary, God and longevity are connected as there is sufficient proof in the writings of many experts that a religious belief enhances the will to live, justifies existence and provides the spiritual support that defeats loneliness.

Thank God, whether you are a believer or an agnostic that recognizes a higher design, for the memories of the loved ones no longer near you, thank him for the good in your life, and for the opportunity to continue living, and most of all for the ability you now have to use your experience of life to carry you further to live longer and achieve fulfillment.

In return for implementing the advice suggested in this e-book, you will be on your way to manage a healthier body, achieve peace of mind and spirit, and for sure you will age elegantly, looking forward to the years ahead.

Good luck.

REFERENCES WEBSITES

http://www.immortalhumans.com

http://www.bioscience.org

http://www.nia.nih.gov/

http://www.longevityforyou.com/

http://en.mimi.hu/environment/carcinogen.ht

http://www.nlm.nih.gov/medlineplus/news/

http://www.naturalantioxidants.org/

http://www.healthyagingandlongevity.com/

http://www.how-to-meditate.org/

http://www.loris.net/thepaperweb.html

http://www.avoidcancernow.com/

http://www.longandwell.com/

http://www.thecentenarian.co.uk/

http://www.yourdnacode.com/antiaging.htm

http://www.hermeticsoft.com/

http://longevity.about.com/

http://www.stemuliteantiaging.com/longevity

http://www.sbsun.com/news/ci_17355775

https://www.eons.com/calculator

http://www.jokebuddha.com/Secret

http://www.sbsun.com/news/ci_17355775

http://www.benbest.com/lifeext/longgene.ht

http://www.attitudefactor.com/

http://news.bbc.co.uk/2/hi/health/8048523.s

http://www.motivatingquotes.com/attitude.ht

http://www.ncbi.nlm.nih.gov/pubmed/26459

http://www.diethealthclub.com/

http://theantiagingnutrition.com/tag/salmon/

http://www.thirdage.com/aging-well

http://www.foodandlife.com/foodd.html

http://healthmad.com/nutrition/

http://www.thecentenarian.co.uk/

http://www.yourdnacode.com/antiaging.htm

http://www.hermeticsoft.com/

http://www.dnai.org/a/

http://www.genome.gov/10001772

Joseph D. Camhi, PhD

www.ingramcontent.com/pod-product-compliance
Lightning Source LLC
Chambersburg PA
CBHW062057280526
45788CB00003B/1269